I dedicate this book
to my wife Lucy,
who saved me
from myself!

Story by Reuben & Lucy Maestas
Drawings by Reuben Maestas

Snidely Shares Some Stories

-

Silly, smiling Snidely
sure says some
super silly sayings.
So, see Snidely
speak some short,
slightly strange,
side-slapping,
simply silly stories.

Summer Solstice
Saturday,
Snidely starts
sharing stories.

Singer songwriter
Snidely sometimes
showcases some sweet
soulful-sounding songs,
starring Snidely,
smooth, slippery,
slinky snake.

Shifting Sideways...

Snidely starts shifting smoothly, swaying south, softly shuffling sand.

Snidely's Sunflower Story

-

Snidely sees
something
so special.
Snidely spots
seven super
stunning,
sweet-smelling,
sun-showered
sunflowers.

See Snidely
sniffing some
sun-shining
sunflowers.
Sniff, sniff, sniff!
Snidely's smelling
some stunningly soft,
strikingly sweet
sssssunflowers!

Snidely says, "Stop!!!" "Smell some sunflowers!"

See seven sunflowers?

13

Snidely's Singing Story

-

Silly smiling
Snidely slid
slowly south,
singing silly summer
solstice songs.

Some say snakes
shouldn't sing.
Snidely says,
"sure, some
snakes sing
silly songs."

See Snidely Singing

-

So, Snidely
starts singing!
"Ssssummer Sunshine,
Ssssweet,
Sweet, Ssssummer
Sunshine."

Singing Snidely Snake...

Snidely's Sun Shade Story

-

Snidely spots
something spectacular!
Snidely sees
someone's sharp,
slick, so stylish,
summer sun shades!
Some say sun shades,
some say shades,
some say sunglasses!

Super Snazzy!

Snidely's Summer Sun Shades

-

Silly smiling
Snidely starts
sporting someone's
sprightly, snappy,
smart, summer
sun shades,
so, so shady!

So Suave!

Snidely's Summer Sunset Story

-

Snidely shuffling
so smoothly
south, sees searing,
scorching summer
solstice sunset
setting **slowly**,
slowly, slowly,
sinking.

23

Silly smiling Snidely
sees several
shining stars.
So, Snidely starts
singing, swaying,
slip-sliding sideways.
Sing, Snidely Sing!
"Sssssssuch ssssshiny,
sssssparkly stars,
ssssshooting, shiny,
sssstars, soooooooo
sleepy."

See Snidely Sleeping

-

See slumbering Snidely, sleeping so soundly. Snidely starts snoring, snoring, snoring

SSSSSSSSS!!!

Snidely's Smoothie Story

-

Sunday's sizzling sun starts shining. Snidely's still sliding south. Starving, skinny Snidely suddenly spots some sugary, sweet, savory snack.

Sweet,
strawberry,
swirl
smoothie.

SWIRL

Snidely starts sipping
so satisfyingly
savory, sweet,
slenderizing,
strawberry swirl
smoothie.
Scrumptious!!!

Sip, sip, slurp, slurp,
slurrrrp, slurrrrrpp!!!

SWIRL

Snidely's Sombrero Story

-

Snidely's still sliding south. Surprisingly, Snidely sees someone's sombrero. Snidely seems so surprised. "Super, super, spiffy, snazzy, sporty sombrero." Snidely's still speaking some simply slithery silly sentences!

Snidely's Singing Spanish Salsa Story

-

Singer Songwriter
Snidely starts singing
spicy Spanish salsa
songs, "Sabado, sabado,
ssssiesta, siestas,
si, si, si, sssssopapilla,
si, si, si, ssssssalsa,
si, si, si, ssssarape,
si, si, si sssssseñorita."

Seriously!!! Silly Snake!

Snidely
starts
seriously
sliding
somewhere
south...

Snidely's Spanish Serape Story

-

Still sliding south,
Snidely starts
scurrying, scoping
someone's
short-sleeved
Spanish-style
serape.
So stylish!

Sizing Spanish Style Serape

-

Snidely starts
stretching slowly,
sizing stylish,
silky smooth,
sleek serape.
Snidely says,
"sharp, so
sophisticated,
so spiffy."

So, Snidely
starts sporting
someone's
Spanish serape.

See Sammy Snail.

Snidely's Stinky Shoe Story

-

So, Snidely starts
slithering, sliding
slowly south;
swaying, shuffling
scattering sand,
strolling sideways.
Suddenly, Snidely,
so startled, spots
something shocking!

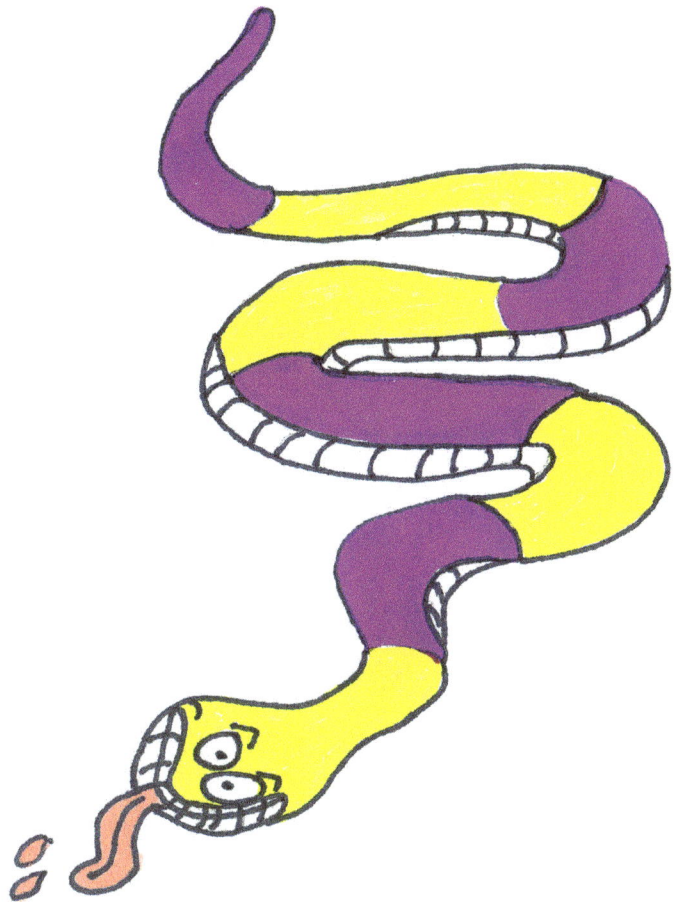

Surprisingly, Snidely spots something sensational, someone's stunningly, striking sienna shoe. Snidely says, "sssssomeone's sssssstinky sssshoe!"

Snidely sees
someone's
single, scrappy,
scruffy, sloppy,
shabbily shaped,
soiled, skunky,
stinky, smelly,
spoiled, sporty
sneaker shoe.

Silly snake sitting sideways, smiling, sizing someone's strange, strong stench, smelly sickening soiled sneaker. Smells so strong. Snidely's stomach starts spinning! Stinky, stinky shoe, sssooo smelly!

Snidely says,
"Ssssmells
ssssooooo
sssstinky."

Snidely's Stylish Story

-

Silly snake, Snidely
sheepishly shows
sporty sun shades,
Spanish sombrero,
summer sunflower,
stylish Spanish serape,
soiled stinky sneaker shoe,
slurping scrumptious
sweet strawberry
swirl smoothie!
So suave, so swanky,
silly, silly snake.

Snidely stages
show-stopping
summer solstice style!

Snazzy,
snazzy
simply silly
snake.

SWIRL

www.ingramcontent.com/pod-product-compliance
Lightning Source LLC
Chambersburg PA
CBHW040256100426
42811CB00011B/1281